MW01138188

The Problem of Poverty

Abraham Kuyper

A translation of the opening address
at the First Christian Social Congress
in the Netherlands, November 9, 1891

Edited and Introduced by **James W. Skillen**

The Center for Public Justice
Washington, DC 20002

BAKER BOOK HOUSE
Grand Rapids, Michigan 49516

Copyright 1991 by
Baker Book House Company

ISBN: 0-8010-5256-4

Second printing, July 1992

Printed in the United States of America

Library of Congress Cataloging-in-Publication Data

Kuyper, Abraham, 1837–1920.
  [Sociale vraagstuk en de Christelijke religie. English]
  The problem of poverty / Abraham Kuyper ; edited by James W.
Skillen.
    p. cm.
  Translation of : Het sociale vraagstuk en de Christelijke religie.
  "A translation of the opening address at the First Christian
Social Congress in the Netherlands, November 9, 1891."
  Includes bibliographical references.
  ISBN 0-8010-5256-4
  1. Church and social problems. 2. Church and the poor.
3. Poverty. 4. Socialism, Christian. I. Skillen, James W.
II. Title.
HN31.K8513 1991
261.8'325–dc20   91-30127
                                                           CIP

Contents

Preface

This speech by Abraham Kuyper, published in Dutch as *Het Sociale Vraagstuk en de Christelijke Religie* [The Social Problem and the Christian Religion] (Amsterdam: J. A. Wormser, 1891), was first translated into English by Dirk Jellema and published as *Christianity and the Class Struggle* (Grand Rapids: Piet Hein, 1950).

The new English version offered here is a thorough revision of Jellema's translation following a careful rereading of the original Dutch. More of Kuyper's long sentences are broken up. Greater sensitivity is shown to contemporary English usage. I have created titles for the four parts of the speech and added sub-headings within each part. The King James Version of the Bible is used for all direct biblical quotations because I feel that it comes the closest to conveying the quality of the language in Kuyper's nineteenth-century Bible.

As is evident from the text, Kuyper is not present-
ing a technical or academic paper. He aims to illumi-
nate a complex problem and to inspire his audience
to action. In a few places, therefore, this translation
takes small liberties with the original Dutch where it
was judged that nothing of substance would be lost
and when the lively spirit of the original seemed to
require a different form of English to convey the
meaning and intent of the original.

I am grateful to Carol Veldman Rudie and Gary
Govert for their critical comments on, and many
helpful suggestions for improving, my first English
draft. They are not to be blamed for any inadequacies
and flaws that remain, but I thank them heartily for
contributing so much to its improvement.

Introduction

The Problem of Poverty
in Centennial Perspective

In 1891, the social implications of the Industrial Revolution were becoming clear throughout much of Europe and America. Rapid urban growth, joblessness, family breakdown, poverty, and social squalor stood out as signs of a severe and growing crisis. In response to this "social problem," as it was frequently called, a new ideology of socialism was gathering steam. Champions of the poor masses, the socialists challenged the political and economic power of industrial capitalists who monopolized the benefits of "progress" for their class. Many feared, and many others hoped for, a new social revolution more radical than the one carried out by the French Revolutionaries a hundred years earlier.[1]

In Europe, a few Christian leaders began to sound an alarm and to take action in Protestant and

Catholic circles. In 1891, Pope Leo XIII released his now-famous encyclical *Rerum novarum,* a forceful call for a Christian solution to the evil distortions of both capitalism and socialism. A group calling itself Christian Socialists was organizing in England. An Evangelical Social Movement was rolling in Germany. Similar movements were emerging in Switzerland, France, and Italy. And, on November 9, 1891, Abraham Kuyper, a leading Dutch statesman, churchman, academic, and journalist, found himself opening the first Christian Social Congress in the Netherlands with an address entitled "The Social Problem and the Christian Religion," retitled here "The Problem of Poverty."[2]

Today, in 1991, talk of an impending socialist revolution may sound oddly out of date. Communist governments in Eastern Europe have collapsed. Socialism in our day appears to be in decline as a political ideology. Liberal democracies and free market capitalism have survived an array of socialist challenges and seem to offer the only viable political and economic hope for the future. Why, at this point in time, would anyone want to reconsider a nineteenth-century discussion of poverty when all evidence suggests that socialism is no longer a revolutionary threat and appears unable to overcome poverty?

While it may be true that various forms of communism and socialism are currently in decline, no one can ignore the present reality of poverty, social dislocation, urban growth and squalor, unemployment, and family breakdown. All of these exist today, throughout the world, on a scale much larger than that of one hundred years ago. Socialism as proposed by Marx, Lenin, Mao Zedong, Stalin, Castro, or even Mikhail Gorbachev may, indeed, have shown itself to be a failure, but the "social problem" is burning today with as much intensity as before.

How, then, shall we answer the question of poverty in our own time? If socialism is not the answer, is capitalism all we have left? What about Christianity? Can we learn anything from the Christian response of one hundred years ago? Across most of Europe today, Christianity appears to be moribund. Is it as dead as socialism appears to be, or does it still have some life? Does *Rerum novarum* or Kuper's speech at the Christian Social Congress of 1891 have any greater potential for inspiring social reform today than Marx's call for a proletarian revolution, or any more vitality than Lenin's appeal to a vanguard of the proletariat to grab political control by revolutionary force?

These questions, it seems to me, are eminently worth testing in this centennial year—worth testing in North America as well as in Poland, the Soviet Union, and Czechoslovakia, worth testing in England and Holland as well as in El Salvador, the Philippines, and Nigeria. Nothing, I believe, could be more timely in 1991, than for socially concerned Christians to read Kuyper's 1891 speech on Christianity and the social problem. This speech not only illuminates with stark simplicity many of the enduring problems of poverty; it also brings a strong and pointed biblical message that has outlived Kuyper's time and place. I doubt that anyone, after reading this speech, can walk away believing that Christianity is out of date and powerless to address the complex questions of poverty today.

Abraham Kuyper

Who was this man called Kuyper? He was born in 1837 in the town of Maassluis, the Netherlands, and was reared in a Reformed (Calvinist) pastor's family. As he matured, he demonstrated considerable intellectual ability and determination, and graduated with highest honors from the famed University of Leiden, where he then earned his doctorate in theology in 1863.[3]

While serving in his first parish as a pastor in a rural village, the bright and confident young man was soon confronted with a personal crisis of faith. Simple people in his congregation helped lead him to a profound and life-changing faith in Jesus Christ. Serving churches in Utrecht and then Amsterdam, the newly inspired Kuyper came under the influence of Protestant political leader Groen van Prinsterer, who himself had undergone a similar conversion in the 1830s.[4] Yielding to Groen's leadership, Kuyper began to devote his considerable intellectual talents to a variety of cultural and political tasks with the aim of encouraging the Christian reformation of church and society.

In 1872, Kuyper became the editor of a new daily newspaper (*De Standaard*), which spoke for the Anti-Revolutionary political movement founded by Groen but not yet organized on a broad, popular basis. By 1879, Kuyper had become the movement's leader and organized it as one of the first mass-democratic parties in Europe. It was the first of what today are known as "Christian Democratic" parties, and Kuyper spent the rest of his life working to show how Christian principles should guide civic action toward the goal of a more just political order. For decades, the Anti-Revolutionary party (ARP) cooperated with Catholic and other Protestant parties in coalition governments, and, as one of the leaders of those cooperative efforts, Kuyper himself served as prime minster of the Netherlands from 1901 to 1905.[5]

Soon after becoming editor of *De Standaard*, Kuyper also took over as editor of a weekly church paper, *De Heraut*, which he served for more than forty-five years. Through both papers, Kuyper sought to educate, inspire, and mobilize Christians in all walks of life to serve God with every talent they possessed. For Kuyper this service obviously embraced journalism, politics, and the church. But that was not all. His theological scholarship was not pushed aside entirely, and he never gave up encouraging Christian reform in the academic realm. In 1880, his efforts along these lines led to the founding of the Free University of Amsterdam, which he served periodically both as a professor and in administrative capacities.[6]

With a full view of his own society and much of Europe—a view made possible by his political, journalistic, ecclesiastical, and academic activities— Kuyper could see by the late 1880s that Protestants in his own country, and European Christians generally, were not adequately rising to the challenge of the growing Industrial Revolution. He therefore worked to organize a Christian social congress that would bring together workers and academics, farmers and church leaders, humble citizens and government leaders, poor and rich, to consider their mutual responsibility for addressing the critical "social problem."

By the end of the nineteenth century, Kuyper's reputation had spread to other parts of the world. He was invited to Princeton University in 1898 to receive an honorary doctorate and to give the annual Stone Lectures, which remain in print to this day.[7] Many of Kuyper's theological writings also were translated.[8] Few of his political writings have been translated, however, partly because they are so much tied to the immediate Dutch political context, and partly because Christian Democratic political movements remain foreign to most of the English-speaking world.[9]

To many North American Christians, Kuyper might appear to be an odd figure. His personal piety was strong but not enclosed in a private sphere. Social and political reform efforts preoccupied him, but they were thoroughly directed by a sense of

Christian calling. He was a theologically trained pastor who nevertheless spent most of his life working in political and journalistic arenas. In one of his devotional books he wrote: "The fellowship of being near unto God must become reality, in the full and vigorous prosecution of our life. It must permeate and give color to our feeling, our perceptions, our sensations, our thinking, our imagining, our willing, our acting, our speaking. It must not stand as a foreign factor in our life, but it must be the passion that breathes throughout our whole existence."[10] This passion to serve God in all areas of life explains the oddity of Abraham Kuyper.

The Framework of Kuyper's Vision

Undergirding the speech translated here is a very definite framework of social and political thought. Two characteristics of that framework are especially important. The first is Kuyper's insight into the tensions and conflicts among competing religions and pseudo-religions in the modern era. The second is his understanding and acceptance of the complex, differentiated character of modern societies.

The Nature of Religion

By far the dominant view of religion in the Western world today is one that associates religion chiefly, if not entirely, with ecclesiastical, theological, and devotional activities and ideas. This is the case in almost all Protestant, Catholic, and Orthodox circles. Religious life is typically defined by a particular set of institutional or cultural expressions, which are then distinguished from "nonreligious" institutions, ideas, and activities. Furthermore, the dominant tendency throughout much of the West for the past two centuries has been to view religion as an old-fashioned hangover from an earlier historical phase of civilization's development. Religion might still hold a certain psychological or political-protest value for some individuals and oppressed peoples, but it is no longer assumed to be meaningful for the shaping of public life in modern, secularized, rationalized, and bureaucratized societies.

Religion, in other words, is generally categorized today as something that certain groups of people *do*—one of the activities they create and pursue. Few Christians, and even fewer non-Christians, think of religion as the totality of what human beings *are*, and what life in this world is all about. That is why most Westerners fail to recognize the religious character of their deepest drives—the driving motives for material prosperity, for national prestige and power, for scientific and technological solutions to life's problems.

Abraham Kuyper thought differently about religion and the complexities of the modern social order.[11] Following his personal conversion, and obviously influenced by Groen van Prinsterer's insight into the religious character of the French Revolution, Kuyper articulated in a profound way the deeper meaning of religion. Religion is not one thing among many that autonomous people choose to do; it is, rather, the direction that human life takes as people give themselves over to the gripping power of either the true God or false gods. Commitments to God or the gods drive and control human life; humans do not control the gods. Religious activities may include worship, prayer, and confession of faith, but such acts do not exhaust religion. At bottom, all of life is religious.

While Kuyper does not discuss the nature of religion at length in his speech, this framework nonetheless controls his argument. That is why he is at pains to contrast a Christian approach to the problem of poverty with liberal and socialist approaches. Ultimately, what is at work in the tension between Christian and non-Christian approaches is not simply disagreements over a few social and economic policies, but a deep opposition between fundamentally different views of life. Kuyper here calls Christians to approach the social problem with all the distinctive resources available to them in the biblical view of God, creation, and especially human nature. Only then will they be able to appreciate the elements of truth to be found in liberalism and socialism.

The Differentiation of Society

A second distinguishing feature of Kuyper's viewpoint is the recognition that God's creation, including the life of society, is meant to unfold and become more complex through historical development.[12] In stressing religion so forthrightly, Kuyper does not speak as a reactionary. He is not one who wants to take his listeners back to an earlier, less complex period of history. He is not decrying industrial development or the emergence of social, academic, and economic institutions that are no longer under control of the church. Rather, he wants to encourage Christians to understand and obey God's guiding principles—God's ordinances—for life in all these diverse spheres of creation. All of life is religious, but not everything is ecclesiastical. All of life must be lived for God, but life is a complex manifold of vocations and responsibilities—no less for Christians than for non-Christians.

In response to the breakdown of medieval Europe's church-centered society and the rise of nationalism, capitalism, and scientific and technological innovation, two secularizing perspectives came to dominate social life and thought in the late nineteenth century: liberal individualism and socialist collectivism. Christians in the Netherlands as well as in other parts of Europe were accommodating themselves to these modes of thought, apparently without realizing how seriously they contradicted basic Christian convictions. In this speech, as in all of his work, Kuyper urges Christians not to retreat into a private faith while giving themselves over in public life to other religious spirits. He wants Christians to live with integrity and to step forward with distinctive contributions to the culture, the economy, political life, education, science, and the art of their day. In the

Netherlands, Kuyper inspired a movement character-
ized by *both* cultural engagement and a nonaccom-
modating Christian approach, *both* the acceptance of
a differentiated social order and the desire to work for
the consistent Christian reform of life in all parts of
society.

Today, the cries for solidarity and integration are
often stronger than those for the differentiation of
society. There are good and important reasons for this
that ought not to be denied or ignored. After all, in
the name of distorted economic and political development, millions of hungry people are denied full access
to society. Millions of people are excluded from real
opportunity because of their skin color, religion, caste,
or gender. These injustices are not expressive of
healthy societal differentiation, and Kuyper nowhere
approves of them. Nevertheless, the appeals for social
solidarity are all too frequently expressive of idola-
trous and utopian aims arising from competing anti-
Christian religions. Kuyper urges social solidarity
(organic social life) in his own country and even internationally, but he does so on a basis that demands
genuine respect for the differentiated integrity of society's many institutions, communities, and social relationships. He sees real dangers in both "social democracy" and "state socialism."

From Kuyper's point of view, there is no short cut
to global integration and human solidarity. Nothing
less than a comprehensive, "architectonic" critique
of society will be sufficient, Kuyper told his audience
in 1891. The same is true today. If Christians are to

contribute to the alleviation of poverty, they will
need to develop a comprehensive Christian social
philosophy. Starting with anything less than an inte-
gral Christian vision will only lead away from the
truth of God's creation order and his sovereignty in
history.

Some Final Clues to the Text

The contemporary reader should have no difficulty
understanding Kuyper's speech. It is neither technical
nor academic. The reader should keep in mind, however, that Kuyper delivered this address one hundred
years ago, at the height of European empire building.
It should not be shocking, therefore, to find him
advocating, in Part 4, European colonization of the
planet as one means of extending and preserving
marriage and family life. Nor should the reader be
surprised by Kuyper's often blunt characterizations of
Catholics, Jews, socialists, and liberals. For all the
blunt talk, these groups learned how to live together
in public life and to cooperate whenever possible.

The reader also should be ready for Kuyper's
repeated reference to the "organic" character of society. There is no doubt that he was influenced by the
romantic and even nationalistic idealism prevalent in
Europe in his day. But one should not jump too
quickly to a false conclusion. Kuyper's argument
shows that his opposition to liberal individualism
was not built upon a collectivist or totalitarian view

of human society. His use of the term "organic" was not intended to reduce individuals to an undifferentiated mass of humanity. Kuyper used the term, together with the idea of diverse spheres of society, to affirm the social character of human life, with its built-in obligations of mutual accountability, trust, and service. Kuyper's critique of socialism, in both its social democratic and state socialist forms, warns of the danger of reducing society to the state or the state to society. The organic character of society can be truly healthy and just only when its real diversity is preserved.

Finally, a word about Kuyper's discussion of socialism. Keep in mind that the year 1891 comes before the era of centralized, communist, Marxist-Leninist governments. The word "socialism," then as now, could be used to refer to several different ideas, schools of thought, and organized political efforts. In fact, in Part 3, Kuyper sorts out several tendencies, distinguishing particularly between "social democracy" and "state socialism." The phrase he uses most frequently throughout the speech is "social democracy," a phrase that refers roughly to what we today would call "democratic socialism." In this translation we have stayed with Kuyper's usage in order not to be anachronistic, although at points we have used the phrase "social-democratic movement" rather than "social democracy" when it seemed more appropriate.

The power of Kuyper's speech on the problem of poverty comes not from any detailed analysis of welfare policies or any novel ideas about labor law or government spending. Rather, its power is derived from a religiously deep insight into the nature of poverty in societies where "organic" wholeness and differentiated freedoms should stand together in expressing the true nature of human beings as the image of God. The enduring value of the speech comes from Kuyper's ability to appeal to deep Christian motives for action, expose the false hopes and illusions raised by secularized revolutionaries and reformers, and envision a better future made possible not by autonomous human activity but by repentance and renewal in accord with God's ordinances of love, mercy, justice, and compassion.

1

*F*acing the *R*eality of *P*overty

think I will be acting in accord with your wishes if, right from the outset in this opening address, I conceive the purpose of our first Congress as modestly as possible. No one should imagine for a moment that we intend to imitate those impressive assemblies where academic specialists from every country of Europe gather to display their wealth of knowledge, or to show off the glitter of their talent. One of the pitiful fruits of state monopoly, which continues to increase in this country's universities, is that we have not yet even produced academic specialists. None of us at this Congress stands out as an expert in economics, for example. But if my interpretation is correct, you have girded yourselves not to cross swords here with the opposition in a public tournament, but to speak together as brothers united in the name of Jesus, and to discuss seriously this question: *What should we, as confessors of Christ, do about the social needs of our time?*

Those who profess Jesus in other lands have also realized the necessity for such action. Recall the appearance of the Christian Workers party in the circle around Count von Waldersee in Berlin. Think of the Christian Socialists, inspired by Maurice and Kingsley, who have united in one group under Rev. Headlam in London. Consider the Swiss Christian Society for Social Economy, organized two years ago in Geneva. And, speaking now of Christianity in the broadest sense, recall what has been done toward a solution of the social problem by such able Catholic thinkers as Le Play and Von Ketteler, by a whole series of momentous Catholic congresses in Germany, France, and Belgium, and most recently by Pope Leo XIII in his encyclical [*Rerum novarum*].[1]

We Have Been Too Slow to Act

So our debut here does not come too early, but too late, and we lag behind others when we could have preceded them. For is it not true that, even before a single voice had been heard among Christians outside the Netherlands, our poets Bilderdijk and Da Costa and statesman Groen van Prinsterer had already called our attention to the social need?

Bilderdijk as early as 1825 addressed the lower classes:

> You sigh and languish in poverty and decay
> While luxury defiantly feasts on the fruit of your
>   own hands.

In face of this need, he ridicules the false doctrine of charity when he introduces traditional liberalism as saying:

> Yes, the land collapses from the poor.
> Why not deport them?
> Then we would be relieved of them.
> It is a bunch of rascals that we pity.
> Who does not find even honest poverty already too
>   expensive?
> They hunger, it is true, they find no work;
> But how can they be of any use, when there is no
>   work for them?

By contrast, Bilderdijk puts his finger on the wound in the opening words of his caustic *Muckrakings*, thereby calling Christians to do penance:

> Whenever a people is destined to perish in sin,
> It's in the church that the soul-leprosy begins.

Fifteen years later, Da Costa, in his *Song of 1840*, lashed out just as ruthlessly at the Plutocracy—the "rule of money" as he called it—and pictured for us the social crisis which was then approaching and is now here:

Here luxury, grown beyond itself, externally healthy
And glittering with youth, but inwardly scorched
And sap-destroying like a cancer, and, as it were,
Destroying the balance between the classes. . . .
   There
Muttering at the work that gives no bread: yokes
Thrown on the neck of the free, where the walls
Burn with heat day and night, and an eternal smoke
Blackens the cities, and the fumes suffocate the soul.

So prophesied Da Costa, who founded his Internationale in London in 1864, a quarter of a century
before Karl Marx. And in 1853, Groen van Prinsterer
frightened the distinguished gentlemen in the Binnen-
hof [seat of Parliament] with his brusque declaration:
"With reference to socialist ideas, one should pay
attention to the truly wretched condition of the lower
classes, especially to the harm which the higher
classes, through their moral corruption and pseudo-
science, have brought about among the people." He
declared that in socialism "there is a measure of truth
mingled with error, which gives it its power." He recognized that "one should also try to improve material
conditions, the injustice of which multiplies the
power of the socialist error." He called upon his fellow
Christians to extinguish the fire when he wrote,
"socialism finds its source in the French Revolution,"
and for that reason, even as the Revolution itself, "can
be conquered only by Christianity."[2]

By now, then, at the late date of this Congress, we
find ourselves fighting a rearguard action. The socialists themselves, and not only our Christian leaders,

expose our failure to act. Socialists constantly invoke
Christ in support of their utopias, and continually hold
before us important texts from the Holy Word. Indeed,
socialists have so strongly felt the bond between social
distress and the Christian religion that they have not
hesitated to present Christ himself as the great
prophet of socialism. They cry out, "there can be no
talk of a failure of Christian liberation; only two mil-
lennia lie between the beginning and the conclusion of
the work undertaken by Christ."[3]

A liberal of the old school, Adolphe Naquet, is consequently uneasy that socialism may be generating
new triumphs for Christianity. He reproaches the
socialist for furthering the cause of religion despite his
hatred for it. "You do the work of religion," he
exclaims, "when you put in the foreground exactly
those problems in whose solution Christianity is so
closely involved." This is an unintentional but nevertheless meaningful tribute to the influence that Christianity can exercise in bringing about a solution of the
social problem. That influence comes out more beautifully in these rich words of Johann Fichte: "Christianity hides in its womb a much greater treasure of
rejuvenation than you suspect. Until now it has
exerted its power only on individual people and only
indirectly on the state. But anyone, whether believer
or unbeliever, who has been able to detect its hidden
power, must grant that Christianity can also exert a
wonderful organizing power on society; and not till
this power bursts through will the religion of the
cross shine before the whole world in all the depths of

its conception and in all the wealth of the blessings which it brings."

Enough has been said, then, my friends, to arouse within you the firm conviction that the direct relationship between the social problem and the Christian religion is simply undeniable. We should feel ashamed that the voice of conscience has not spoken more loudly within us before now, or at least that it did not stir us to earlier action. We should feel humiliated that, in the face of so crying a need, we have not long since been acting in the name of Jesus. In this spirit of self-criticism I can understand your reproach that an obvious truth like this need not even be demonstrated in a gathering such as this. Standing before the agonizing distress of these times, a distress which at every point is related to the very essence of error and sin, our eye should not be allowed, nor should it be able, to turn away from the *Christus Consolator* [Christ the Consoler], who assuredly addresses our violently disturbed century with the persistent call of his divine compassion: "Come *to me*, wealthiest century in history, which is so deathly weary and heavy laden, and *I* will give you rest."

The Relationship of Christianity to the Problem of Poverty

Therefore, on the existence of this relationship [between Christianity and the social problem] I shall not waste another word. Recognition of it is indeed the presupposition of this Congress. But what you *do* expect of me, and, with your indulgence, what I will at least *try* to furnish, is a laying bare of the threads by which these two phenomena are intertwined. Our conviction that such a relation exists is not enough. It must also take on form and shape. Only then can it speak to us.[4]

I select as point of departure a contrast that is plain for all to see. I mean the contrast between *nature*, as it exists independent of our will, and our human *art*, which acts on nature. The whole social problem is born of the relationship between human life and the material world that surrounds us. Now, in human life as well as in the material world there is on the one hand a power beyond our reach that we commonly call nature, and on the other hand there is a power originating in the human will that we may refer to simply as art. Our human nature is placed in the wider nature around us, not to leave it untouched, but, by an urge and calling within us, to work on nature through human art, to ennoble and perfect it. An example is the breeding of horses for the improvement of the strain. Another can be found in the work of the competent florist who does not gather a bouquet of wild flowers but rather increases and refines varieties through the mingling of seeds. Steam comes from water. Out of the dull stone comes the sparkling diamond. Men lead the wild stream that tumbles down the mountains into safer channels, to make its water serve for shipping and for irrigating fields.

Briefly, then, human art acts on every part of nature, not to destroy it or simply to impose another structure alongside it, but to unlock the power that lies hidden within it or to regulate the wild power that springs from it. God's ordinances require this. While still in paradise man received the order "to preserve and cultivate" the material world. It was created—forgive me here the indispensable Germanism—to be "completely perfected." Every creature, our Confession says so beautifully, must serve man, so that man may serve his God.

This rule also certainly applies in both the personal and social aspects of human life. It is a renunciation of duty when you let your inner nature run its course unbridled, without coming to its rescue to improve it through the holy art of "watching, praying, and struggling." It is shameful for fathers and mothers to let their children grow up naturally without improving on nature through the art of education. It is nothing but primitive barbarism whenever human society, without higher supervision, is left to the course of nature. Thus, the art of statecraft, here taken in the higher sense, intervenes so that out of society a community may develop, and that the community, both in itself and in its relation to the material world, may be ennobled.

If, in the course of history, men did not fall into error, if egoism and crime did not interfere, then the development of human society would always follow

its course peacefully, moving forward without inter-
ruption to a completely happy condition. Unfortu-
nately, the situation is not so promising. True, a certain instinct has guided every culture to the
recognition of a few indispensable bases for all
human society. In this respect, geniuses and heroic
figures have from ancient times had many a fortunate intuition. But as soon as it came to the need for
a more elaborate regulation of this complex phenomenon which we call human society, action after
action was misdirected, as much by those who established social customs as by those who acted with
magisterial power.

Human Error and Sin

In both instances the series of misdirected actions
had two invariable causes: error and sin. *Error* insofar
as there was ignorance about the essence of man and
his social attributes, as well as about the laws that
govern human association and the production, distribution, and use of material goods. *Sin* insofar as greed
and lust for power (expressed either through force or
through vicious custom and unjust law) disturbed or
checked the healthy growth of human society, sometimes cultivating a very cancerous development for
centuries. In time, both error and sin joined forces to
enthrone false principles that violated human nature.
Out of these false principles systems were built that
varnished over injustice and stamped as normal that

which actually stood opposed to the requirements for
life.

This reckless play with human society was carried
on at all times and among all peoples. It was carried
on by intellectuals and by proprietors in private life,
and eventually, under their inspiration, by governments in an equally irresponsible fashion. It is perfectly true that the social problem in the narrower
sense comes up for discussion only at scattered inter-
vals, with the consequence that many are under the
delusion that the intervention of government in
social affairs is a novelty of our times. Actually, however, there has never been a government in any country of the world which did not in various ways govern
the course of social life and its relationship to material wealth. Governments have done this directly
through a variety of regulations in civil law and trade
law, and indirectly through constitutional law and
criminal law. More particularly, governments have
acted through inheritance laws, systems of taxation,
export and import regulations, codes for purchase and
rent, agrarian regulations, colonial administration,
control of coinage, and much more. It has never been
possible to speak of a wholly free and instinctive
growth of society in any country with a high degree of
national development. Everywhere, human art has
shaped the development of natural powers and relationships. But while we must gratefully acknowledge
that this intervention of human management has
brought us, generally speaking, out of barbarism into
an orderly society—indeed, although we must con-

cede that such a continuous development of society strengthens belief in a higher providential rule—we cannot for a moment doubt that this intervention, often originating from false principles, has in all ages created unhealthy conditions which could have been healthy. It has in many ways poisoned our mutual relationships and weighed us down with nameless misery.[5]

The ineradicable inequality between men produced a world in which the stronger devours the weaker, much as if we lived in an animal society rather than in a human society. The stronger, almost without exception, have always known how to bend every custom and magisterial ordinance so that the profit is theirs and the loss belongs to the weaker. Men did not literally eat each other like cannibals, but the more powerful exploited the weaker by means of a weapon against which there was no defense. And whenever the magistrate came forward as a servant of God to protect the weak, the more powerful class of society soon knew how to exercise such an overpowering influence that the government, which should have protected the weak, became an instrument against them. This was not because the stronger class was more evil at heart than the weaker, for no sooner did a man from the lower class rise to the top than he in his turn took part just as harshly—yes, even more harshly—in the wicked oppression of those who were members of his own former class. No, the cause of evil lay in this: that men regarded humanity as cut off from its eternal destiny, did not honor it as created in the image of God, and did not reckon with the majesty of the Lord, who alone by his grace is able to hold in check a human race mired in sin.

This unjust situation was already born in ancient times, of which the Preacher so movingly complains: "So I returned, and considered all the oppressions that are done under the sun: and behold the tears of such as were oppressed, and they had no comforter; and on the side of their oppressors there was power; but they had no comforter" (Eccles. 4:1).[6] The situation is like that when Naboth was murdered so Jezebel could add his acre to the royal park of Ahab (1 Kings 21:1–16). Or, if you will, it is like the state of affairs once and for all identified by our Lord in the parable of the rich man and poor Lazarus (Luke 16:19–31) against which James hurls his apostolic condemnation when he writes: "Go to now, ye rich men, weep and howl for your miseries that shall come upon you. Your riches are corrupted, and your garments are moth-eaten. Your gold and silver is cankered; and the rust of them shall be a witness against you, and shall eat your flesh as it were fire. Ye have heaped treasure together for the last days. Behold, the hire of the laborers who have reaped down your fields, which is of you kept back by fraud, crieth: and the cries of them which have reaped are entered into the ears of the Lord of Sabaoth" (James 5:1–4).[7]

2

Jesus and the Social Problem

ould it be that the Christian faith, having entered the world, would take no stand against such an evil state of affairs? Surely you know that social conditions in Jesus' time—conditions even worse than those that keep contemporary Europe and America in a state of tension—prophesied the approaching fall of the Roman Empire. A genuinely Asiatic despotism was responsible for a system of extortion and exhaustion in almost every province, against which oratorical heroes such as Cicero protested in vain. Then, just as now, the balance between the classes was lost: defiant luxury existed alongside crying poverty, immense accumulations of capital alongside beggarly poverty concealed in the slums of Rome. Corruption in government followed inevitably from these conditions. Sensuality rather than morality set the tone for public opinion. The masses, carried away by need and passion, stood ready at any time to rebel, murder, and plunder.

Jesus—More Than a Social Reformer

Dour, pagan Rome then sank away, as did laughing Greece, into the morass of human misery.[1] But before it sank, a light arose in Bethlehem, a dying cry was heard from Golgotha, and through them a new hope was awakened for all peoples. A new hope, not as might be felt by those who today degrade the Christ of God by casting him as a mere social reformer, but the kind of hope inspired by the *Savior of the World*, which was his higher, richer, and more honorable title. The blessedness that he brought to humanity contained a promise not only for the future but also for the present life (1 Tim. 4:8), although Jesus always emphasized the primacy of man's *eternal* welfare. Soul and body must not be corrupted in hell. The worm that never dies, the wailing and gnashing of teeth in a fire that will never be extinguished—these were the terrors that Jesus saw when he looked at poor humanity; these were the nightmares that gave him no rest. The joy to which he called people had to be the eternal joy of his kingdom. The cruelty of the socialist was never found in

our Savior. For the sake of bettering the lot of
humanity in this short span of temporal existence,
the socialist wildly and recklessly cuts off every
prospect of a glory that shall be eternal.[2] Jesus and his
apostles never preached revolution. We are to submit
to every constituted authority set over us. Poor
Lazarus shall have his revenge, not while he is living
from the crumbs that fall from the rich man's table,
but when the rich man suffers in eternal pain and
poor Lazarus is comforted (Luke 16:19–31).

If then you ask what Jesus did to bring deliverance
from the social needs of his time, here is the answer.
He knew that such desperate needs grow from the
malignant roots of error and sin, so he placed the
truth over against error and broke the power of sin by
shedding his blood and pouring out his Holy Spirit on
his own. Since rich and poor had become divided
because they had lost their point of union in God, he
called both together back to their Father who is in
heaven.[3] He saw how the idolizing of money had
killed nobility in the human heart, so he held up the
"service of Mammon" before his followers as an
object for their deep contempt. Since he understood
the curse that lies in capital, especially for the man of
great wealth, he adjured him to cease his accumulation of capital and to gather not treasure on earth,
where moth and rust corrupt and thieves break in and
steal (Matt. 6:19). He rejected the rich young man
because he could not decide to sell all his goods and
give to the poor. In his heart Jesus harbored no hatred
for the rich, but rather a deep compassion for their

pitiable condition. The service of Mammon is exceedingly difficult. Sooner would a camel go through the eye of a needle than would a rich man enter the kingdom of heaven (Matt. 19:16–24). Only when the possession of money leads to usury and harshness does Jesus become angry, and in a moving parable he tells how the man who would not release his debtor is handed over to torturers and branded as a wicked servant who knows no pity (Matt. 18:23–35).

By Personal Example

Furthermore, Jesus did not limit his work to moral motivation. He also preached by the way he lived. When rich and poor stood opposed to one another, he never took his place with the wealthier but always with the poorer. He was born in a stable; and while foxes have holes and birds have nests, the Son of Man had nowhere to lay his head. His apostles were to give no consideration to the accumulation of capital. They were to go out without purse and without food. While one among them did carry the purse, that one was Judas, the terrible man, who sold his soul to the devil because he was seduced by the love of money.[4] Powerful is the trait of compassion, imprinted on every page of the Gospel where Jesus came into contact with the suffering and the oppressed. He did not push aside the masses who were ignorant of the law, but drew them to himself. He extinguished no wick that was even barely smoldering. He cured the sick. He did not shy away from touching leprous flesh. When the crowds were hungry, even though as yet they did not hunger for the bread of life, he broke the loaf into many pieces and gave them an abundance of precious fish. Jesus practiced what he preached.

The prayer of the writer of Proverbs (30:8) set the tone for Jesus' teaching: "give me neither poverty nor riches; feed me with food convenient for me." From this prayer the apostle deduces a practical lesson for the avaricious man (1 Tim. 6:7–11): "For we brought nothing into this world, and it is certain we can carry nothing out. And having food and raiment let us be therewith content. But they that will be rich fall into temptation and a snare, and into many foolish and hurtful lusts, which drown men in destruction and perdition. For the love of money is the root of all evil. . . . But thou, O man of God, flee these things."

From Jesus' perspective it also follows that the poor man should neither grumble nor let himself be spurred on to bitterness. The poor man should not say in his anxiety, "What shall I eat, and what shall I drink, and what shall I wear?" (cf. Matt. 6:25). Jesus says, "(For after all these things do the Gentiles seek:) for your heavenly Father knoweth that ye have need of all these things" (Matt. 6:32). But he then says something that the socialists so flatly reverse when they preach it: "But seek ye first the kingdom of God, and his righteousness; and all these things shall be added unto you" (Matt. 6:33). Thus, for both rich and poor, Jesus' teaching simultaneously cuts to the root of sin in our human heart.[5]

Jesus also follows up the teaching with his own heart-winning practice of devotion, self-denial, and abundant compassion which pours every ounce of balm at his disposal into the wounds of suffering mankind. In the end he even volunteers himself to the slaughter—for the redemption of both rich and poor—like a Lamb that is dumb before its shearer.

Organizing the Church

Such a presence, such a preaching, such a death, certainly would have been enough in themselves to exercise an influence for good in social relations. The overthrow of the idol Mammon and the refocusing of life's purpose from earth to heaven would, alone, have revolutionized popular consciousness.

But Jesus did not stop here. He also *organized*. He set apart and sent out his church among the nations to influence society in three ways. The first and most important influence was through the *ministry of the Word*, insofar as the Word constantly fights against lust for money, comforts the poor and oppressed, and points to an endless glory that will be exchanged for the suffering of the present time. The church's second influence was through an organized *ministry of charity*, which in the name of the Lord—the single owner of all goods—demands that goods be shared so that no man or woman in the circle of believers is allowed to suffer want or go without necessary

apparel. Third, the church influenced society by
instituting the *equality of brotherhood* (in contrast
to differences in rank and station) both by abolishing
all artificial demarcations between men and by join-
ing rich and poor in one holy food at the Lord's Sup-
per. The communion service is a symbol of the unity
that binds us together not only in our common
humanity but, more important, as those who have
collapsed under the same guilt and have been saved
by the same sacrifice in Christ.[6]

Indeed, as a direct consequence of Christ's appearance and the extension of his church among the
nations, society became markedly different from what
it was in the pagan era. The Roman society of that
time was strikingly like what Jesus once called
"whited sepulchres, which indeed appear beautiful
outward, but are within full of dead men's bones"
(Matt. 23:27). The whited sepulchure of Rome crashed
into ruins. And without claiming that the new social
order, which arose almost spontaneously from that
heap of ruins, corresponded in any sense to the ideal
cherished by Jesus, yet we may gratefully acknowledge that more tolerable social conditions were born.
Earthly welfare no longer weighed heaviest in public
estimation; eternal well-being also carried weight.
Slavery was snapped at its root and underwent a
moral criticism that sapped it as an institution. Men
began to be concerned about caring for the poor and
for orphans. Accumulation of too much capital was
checked by the prohibition of usury. Higher and lower
classes approached each other more freely on a more

equal footing. The contrast of abundance and scarcity was not erased, but extreme luxury no longer clashed so sharply with dire poverty. Man had not yet arrived at the point where he should be, but at least he was started along a better path; and had the church not gone astray from her simplicity and her heavenly ideal, the influence of the Christian religion on political life and social relationships would eventually have become dominant.

The Christianization of Europe occurred too quickly, however, and the diverse groups of people that had to be assimilated were altogether too massive. Constantine's conversion became, for the church, the signal to wed itself to the power of the world, thereby cutting the nerve of her strength. From then on, as a consequence, the world gradually crept into the church. Instead of disciples who went without purse or food, richly endowed princes of the church housed themselves in magnificent palaces. As successors of the Galilean fisherman at the head of the church in Rome, a series of popes displayed royal pomp. A Julius II or a Leo X seemed more bent on paganizing Christianity than on Christianizing worldly life.[7] The salt lost its savor, and social corruption regained its ancient strength—a corruption checked but not brought under control in the lands of the Reformation. And in those parts of Europe that remained Catholic, royal absolutism and aristocratic pride created conditions for the ripening of an unbearable social tension that eventually brought forth the French Revolution.

3

The Socialist Challenge

The French Revolution, against which every Christian who thinks consistently should turn, produced its evil not so much by throwing the Bourbons from the throne, nor by making the middle class more powerful than both the nobility and the clergy, but rather by completely changing people's consciousness and view of life.

In the Christian religion, authority and freedom are bound together by the deeper principle that everything in creation is subject to God. The French Revolution threw out the majesty of the Lord in order to construct an artificial authority based on individual free will. That project resembled a scaffold nailed together from odd planks and beams,

which cracks and falls when the first gale rises. The
Christian religion teaches us that life on earth is part
of an eternal existence. The French Revolution, by
contrast, denied and opposed everything beyond the
horizon of this earthly life. The Christian religion
speaks of a lost paradise, a state of purity from
which we fell, and for that reason calls us to humil-
ity and conversion. The French Revolution saw in
the state of nature the criterion of what is normally
human, incited us to pride, and substituted the lib-
eralizing of man's spirit for the need of conversion.
Springing from God's love, the Christian religion
brings loving compassion into the world. Over
against that compassion, the French Revolution
placed the egoism of a passionate struggle for possessions. And finally, to touch on the real point that
lies at the heart of the social problem, the Christian
religion seeks personal human dignity in the social
relationships of an organically integrated society.
The French Revolution disturbed that organic tissue,
broke those social bonds, and left nothing but the
monotonous, self-seeking individual asserting his
own self-sufficiency.[1]

With this the die was cast. By wrenching loose
everything that held life together in human dignity,
it was inevitable that a profound *social need* would
be born, followed by the emergence of a widespread
social-democratic movement, and then by an ex-
tremely knotty *social question* that would confront
every nation. I do not deny that the application of
steam to machinery, along with faster communica-

tion between countries and rapid population growth,
contributed to the worsening of social relationships.[2]
But I firmly believe that neither the social question,
which now holds two continents in feverish tension,
nor the social-democratic movement, which now
threatens the public order in Europe and America,
would ever have assumed such ominous proportions
if the French Revolution had not brought about such
a complete change in the consciousness of nations,
classes, and the individual.[3]

Social Need

In the first place, then, the French Revolution, by
its very nature, produced a deep-seated social need. It
made the possession of money the highest good, and
then, in the struggle for money, it set every man
against every other. This is not to say that the scram-
ble for money was published in the Revolution's program, or that its more inspired spokesmen did not
coax more noble sounds from their harps. But the
theory, the system, inevitably resulted in a kneeling
before Mammon because it cut off the horizon of
eternal life. It compelled men to seek happiness on
earth, in earthly things, and thus created a sphere of
lower pressures in which money was the standard of
value, so that everything was sacrificed for money.
Now add the demolition of all social organization,
followed by proclamation of the mercantile gospel of
laissez faire, and you can understand how the "strug-

gle for life" was ushered in by the "struggle for money." The law of the animal world—dog eat dog—became the basic law for every social relationship. The love of money, the holy apostle taught us, is the root of all evil. As soon as that evil demon was unchained at the turn of the century, no consideration was shrewd enough, no strategy crafty enough, no deception outrageous enough among those who, through superiority of knowledge, position, and capital, took money—and ever more money—from the socially weaker.

This condition would have existed even if the opportunities at the beginning of the struggle had been equal for both parties. It became worse by degrees because the opportunities at the start were so obviously unequal. On the side of the bourgeosie there was experience and insight, ability and association, available money and available influence. On the side of the rural population and the working class, which were destitute of knowledge and deprived of all resources, the daily need for food forced men to accept any condition, no matter how unjust.[4] Even without prophetic gifts, one could foresee the outcome of this struggle. It could not end otherwise than in the absorption of all excess value by the larger and smaller capitalists, leaving for the broader strata of society only as much as seemed absolutely necessary to maintain them as instruments for nourishing capital. For in this system that is precisely what the workers are considered to be—instruments, tools. Thus, a social condition found previously only among

the Jews—"at one end of the social scale, millionaires;
at the other, ant-poor drudges"—has gradually come
to exist throughout Europe, but now without the pal-
liatives of family ties and compassion for poverty-
stricken co-religionists that had an ameliorating effect
among our Jewish fellow-citizens.[5] Thus, in all of
Europe a well-to-do bourgeoisie rules over an impover-
ished working class, which exists to increase the
wealth of the ruling class and is doomed, when it can
no longer serve that purpose, to sink away into the
morass of the proletariat.

The social need is worsened by the fact that the
luxurious bourgeoisie makes a display of its luxury,
exciting a false desire in the poorer classes. By undermining the kind of contentment often exhibited by
those who possess little, the bourgeoisie ignites the
poor man's feverish passion for pleasure.[6]

Social Democracy

With equally rigorous necessity, that same system
gave birth, in the second place, to a social-democratic
movement, with its open proclamation of a coming
revolution. The French Revolution had written on its
blood-red banner not only "freedom" but also "equality and fraternity," and it was certainly not least the
French farmers and workers who in the wars of the
French Republic rushed to the battlefields, singing
the Marseillaise, to seize these precious ideals. Alas,
the equality of which men had dreamed turned out

to be an even more offensive inequality. Instead of the promised fraternity, they got a modern performance of the fable of the wolf and the lamb.

Was it not inevitable, therefore, that from this suffering class of society a very natural question would arise: "With what right do men force on us this desperate poverty? We were taught that we are as good as anyone else, and that the minority should subject itself to the majority. Well, are we not the majority, the huge majority, the overwhelming masses? Is it not a violation of the principles of the French Revolution, and a mockery of the sacred rallying cry for which so much blood flowed in Paris, that a new aristocracy, an aristocracy of much lower calibre—an *aristocracy of money*—sets itself up to lay down the law to us, to put its foot on our neck, and thus to reinstate the same evil overthrown by the almost unbelievable exertions of the Voltaires and Rousseaus and the heroes of the Bastille? Give us what is coming to us—our proper role in the program of the French Revolution. Then we will outvote you and furnish you with a wholly new social system that will give the death blow to privilege forever. Then, finally, we will have for ourselves what your pretty theory promised but which you never granted us."

In all seriousness, I do not see how anyone who supports the theory of the French Revolution can, on logical grounds, object to this demand from social democrats. From that standpoint, I for one must agree unconditionally with them. Once the false theory is granted, social democracy and it alone is consistent.[7] Nor do I see how social democracy can be condemned in the name of the French Revolution by objecting that it errs in openly preaching revolution and insisting that, if necessary, it will not hold back from violence. Did the distinguished gentlemen from the circle of the Girondins preach no violence? Did men treat Louis XVI courteously because of a principle that the social order should *not* be broken? Did the spiritual forefathers of our liberals and conservatives shrink back from violence in the September murders? To raise these questions is to lapse into absurdity as long as the dull rumble of the guillotine still echoes tragically and restlessly in our ears, and when so recently the centennial of the storming of the Bastille was celebrated by all of liberal Europe as the commemoration of a praiseworthy and heroic feat. How can those, who have themselves not hesitated to wade through streams of blood to reach their goal, abandon others in contempt when they too, in a tight corner, would consider erecting the guillotine?

I naturally shudder as I utter these words. Everything that the Christian religion teaches stands in horrified opposition to such words. But, comparing the social democrat to the liberal, I neither can nor may blame him. It is to use a double standard, it is hypocrisy or self-deception, for those who themselves were born of the Revolution—yes, from regicide—to count it a mortal sin in their own spiritual children when they too dare to speak of "forceful means."[8]

The Social Question

Next I come to a more attractive subject. For the French Revolution gave birth to a third consequence, this time by way of reaction. I do not now refer to social need or social democracy, but to the social question. The social question did not, of course, present itself here for the first time. It was under discussion in ancient history, as much on the Euphrates as on the Tiber, as much in Sparta as in Athens. The social question emerged again when the feudal system found acceptance, and again centuries later when it passed away. To give an example from our own Dutch history, the social question was resolved twice in Java, first with the introduction and then with the abolition of our cultural system.

Whenever one uses the phrase "social question," one recognizes, in the most general sense, that serious doubt has arisen about the *soundness of the social structure in which we live*. One thereby acknowledges that public opinion is at war over the foundation on which a more appropriate—and therefore more liveable—social order may be built.[9] Merely to pose the question in no way implies that it has to be answered in a *socialistic* manner. The solution one reaches can be of a totally different kind. Only one thing is necessary if the social question is to exist for you: you must realize the untenability of the present state of affairs, and you must account for this untenability not by incidental causes but by a fault in the very foundation of our society's organization. If you do not acknowledge this and think that social evil can be exorcised through an increase in piety, or through friendlier treatment or more generous charity, then you may believe that we face a religious question or possibly a philanthropic question, but you will not recognize the *social* question.[10] This question does not exist for you until you exercise an architechtonic critique of human society, which leads to the desire for a different arrangement of the social order.

With regard to the untenability of the present circumstances, spawned as they have been by the individualism of the French Revolution, I think there can be little difference of opinion among Christians. As long as you still feel a human heart beat within you, and as long as the ideal of our holy gospel inspires you, then every higher aspiration you have must clash with the current state of affairs. Obviously, if social developments continue to follow the present course, life on earth will become less and less a heaven and more and more a hell. Our society is losing touch with Christ; it lies in the dust bowed down before Mammon. The very foundations of the earth tremble (as the psalmist would complain) from the relentless goad of the most brutal egoism (Pss. 11:3; 82:5). All tie-beams and anchors of the social structure are shifting; disorganization breeds demoralization; and in the increasing wantonness of some people contrasted with the steadily increasing need of others, you detect something of the decomposition of a corpse rather than the fresh bloom and muscular strength of sound health.[11]

No, it need not remain so. It can become better. And improvement undoubtedly lies—I do not shrink from the word—along a *socialistic* path, provided that you do not mean by "socialistic" the program of the social democrats, but merely the idea, in itself so beautiful, that our national society is, as Da Costa said, "not a heap of souls on a piece of ground," but rather a God-willed *community*, a living, human organism. Not a mechanism put together from separate parts; not a mosaic, as Beets has called it, inlaid with pieces like a floor; but a *body* with limbs, subject to the law of life. We are members of each other, and thus the eye cannot get along without the foot, nor the foot without the eye. It is this human, this scientific, this Christian truth that, because of the French Revolution, people failed to recognize, stoutly denied, and so grievously assailed. Against the individualism of the French Revolution, born from its denial of human community, the whole movement of society in our times is now turning.[12]

Socialism Is No Temporary Fad

You are mistaken, then, if you think that contemporary socialism has its source in the confused utopias of fanatics, or was born in the minds of starving hotheads. Karl Marlo, who in three thick volumes first proposed the "organization of labor," was a preeminently able professor. Johan Karl Rodbertus, who pleaded for the social question prior to Karl Marx, was minister of the king of Prussia in 1848. Marx himself, the founder of the Internationale, belonged to the highest class and married into a ministerial family. Lasalle moved in the circles of *le haute monde*. Henry George was an American of the best class. Albert Schaeffle, who wants to go so far as to turn over land, tools, *and capital* to collective control, was minister of the emperor of Austria in 1871. The thoughtful person can hardly restrain a certain Homeric laugh when he recalls talk (in our own circles until quite recently) of socialism as something peculiar to the riffraff. One wonders whether people still read, whether they are in tune with the times. Did H. P. G. Quack knock at the door of the deaf when he introduced in such enthralling words the whole socialist family to our cultured public? Have people never heard that Plato, the greatest philosopher of Greece, wrote about and recommended a plan for a completely socialistic arrangement of the state? If such extreme ignorance about socialist designs was excusable twenty years ago, it now leads only to obscurantist politics.

Today the socialist movement has taken shape in four different scientific schools. Spontaneously and simultaneously, in every land of Europe, it has startled the contented bourgeosie from their tranquility. Socialism finds advocates in a whole series of universities and makes the presses groan under a constant stream of studies. It has gradually acquired such

depth, extension, and increased significance that Bis-
mark himself joined the movement, Pope Leo XIII
sent out an encyclical about it, and the emperor of
Germany even began his reign with a congress in the
capital of Prussia to prepare for an international solution of the social question.[13] Certainly, no head-in-
the-sand politics will be of any avail here. It will do
no good to scoff at "justice for all," to declare
Domela Nieuwenhuis socially outcast, and to let the
stupid crowd sing about all the "socialists in a her-
ring barrel." Socialism is in the air. The social wind,
which can at any moment change to a storm, bulges
the sails of the political ship. It may safely be said
that the social question has become *the* question, the
burning *life-question,* of the late nineteenth century.
Indeed, in the whole of this century, so prodigally
rich in problems, no other problem has emerged that
reaches so deeply into the lives of the nations and
agitates public opinion with such ferocity.[14]

The common characteristic of this imposing
movement is to be found in the swelling of community feeling—feeling for social justice and for the
organic nature of society—over against the one-
dimensional individualism of the French Revolution
and its corresponding economic school of laissez
faire. The battle over proprietary rights and against
capitalism is merely a consequence of this zealous-
ness for the social principle, inasmuch as it is precisely in the absolute right of property that the individual finds his strongest bulwark. By virtue of
absolute ownership, immeasurable fortunes were

heaped up, producing an insurmountable obstacle
that hinders society from doing justice to its own
sociological character.[15]

The Unity and Divisions of Socialism

In its opposition to individualism, therefore, the
socialist movement in all its branches is united.
However, as soon as the question is raised about
what should be demolished and what should take its
place, there are as many opinions as there are people.
Obviously, if one does not believe in a God before
whose eternal ordinances men must bow; if one does
not see in the life of the nation a historical development that never permits its intrinsic law of life to be
violated with impunity; if one sees in all the struc-
tures of our present society only the product of arbitrary human will; then, in consequence, one will feel
justified in overthrowing everything that hinders the
gigantic task of building anew on the vacant plot.

Among those who think along these lines, the
most radical is the nihilist, who, seeing how human
life is totally interdependent, expects no salvation as
long as anything remains of a civilization that has
died. For that reason he wants to begin by destroying
everything, literally everything. His ideal is to go
back to the time right after the flood. For him the
center of gravity lies in the *nothing*.

Less radical than the nihilist is the anarchist, who
ridicules the nihilist's view of things—as though the

virus could cling to houses and tools! He sees the poison only in government and in every function and power that emanates from government. For him the demolition will have gone far enough if every government is elminated. No more state; only a society. Then the golden age will arise of its own accord.

Still less radical are the social democrats, who want to hold on to both state and society, but a state that will be merely the housekeeper of society. The state ought to "keep house" so that the many family households will dissolve themselves into the single household of the state. In this single household, every citizen should share equally without distinction. Of course, among these men you find variations: fanatics without scruples, preaching plunder and insurrection, alongside men like Liebknecht who seek salvation in parliamentary triumphs. Schaeffle, who would collectivize land, tools, and capital, stands alongside the ordinary collectivist who would have the state own only the land and the tools. But in the end they all reach the same conclusion: the single state swallowing up every individual and caring for every individual equally.

At a fair distance from the social democrats you find the state socialists, who, although they may include variant forms, reverse the above position and place the authority of the state high *above* society. They ascribe to state authority the task of leading society patriarchally. This school has found enthusiastic spokesmen in Rudolph Meyer, A. H. G. Wagner, and partly in Laveleye and many others, and has finally found its ideal statesman in Bismarck. The power of the historical school lies less in a practical program than in scientific research directed against the illusion that the present social situation and legal relationships have an absolute character. It thus prepares public opinion for modification of the existing state of affairs, and tries to discover the law for such alterations.

Add to this list the less doctrinaire liberals for whom there is an increasingly noticeable inclination, on the one hand, to become more conservative—that is, to make concessions necessary to conserve the present situation—and, on the other hand, to become more radical by strengthening the political influence of the lower class in order to improve its lot and to curtail the endangered privileges of the propertied class.

To complete this brief summary I must finally add to the list the cynical pessimists, who see that some mischief is smouldering in the household of modern civilization and even concede that there is a fire. They admit that unless that fire is checked, the flame of an all-destroying revolution will soon break out. But they contend that to extinguish the fire is simply impossible. Therefore, they prophesy with stoic calm that our modern civilization, like the Oriental and Graeco-Roman civilizations, is destined to go down into Nirvana.[16]

4

A Christian Approach to the *Problem of Poverty*

If I am not mistaken, this hasty sketch has revealed the threads by which the Christian religion must be woven together with the social problem. All that remains, therefore, is to pick up these threads one by one in order to show you the direction they ought to give to our study and action.

We must, however, first clear up a question which, if left unanswered, would probably nullify the force of my argument. That question is this: How can I call social democracy a fruit of the French Revolution and at the same time assert that it is opposed and hostile to the principle of the French Revolution?

This apparent contradiction arises from the fact that the individualistic character of the French Revolution is only a *derived* principle. Individualism is not the *root* principle from which the Revolution gains its dynamic. The root principle for the French Revolution is its God-provoking cry "neither God, nor master"—the ideal of humanity emancipated from God and from his established order. From this principle extend two lines, not just one. The first is the line along which you move in making up your mind to break down the established order of things, leaving nothing but the individual with his own free will and imaginary supremacy. Alongside this runs another line, at the end of which you are tempted not only to push aside God and his order, but also (now deifying yourself) to sit on God's throne, as the prophet said, and to create a new order of things out of your own brain. This last is what social democracy wants to do. There is, in this aim, no letting go of the individualistic starting point. In fact, social democracy wants to erect a social structure (by means of universal suffrage) on the foundation of the sovereignty of the people, and thus on individual will.[1]

Response to Socialism

But that is only in passing. The question that now requires our full attention is this: *What attitude should those who profess the Christian religion assume toward this socialist movement?*

Certainly the general collapse of our social life and the human need that results from it arouse our deep compassion. We may not, as the priest and the Levite, pass by the exhausted traveler who lies bleeding from his wounds. Rather, we must, like the merciful Samaritan, be deeply moved by a divine sympathy—because suffering exists, because there is a crying need. That need is perhaps not yet so great in the circles of our regular tradespeople, but it certainly exists among the proletariat who stand behind them, as well as among some in the rural areas. Think of Friesland. Then I too say with Bilderdijk, God has not willed that one should drudge hard and yet have no bread for himself and his family. Still less has God willed that any man with hands to work and a will to work should perish from hunger or be reduced to the beggar's staff just because there is no work.[2]

If we have food and clothing, then the holy apostle demands that we should content ourselves with that. But where our Father in heaven wills with divine generosity that an abundance of food grows from the ground, we are without excuse if, through our fault, this rich bounty is divided so unequally that one is surfeited with bread while another goes with an empty stomach to his pallet, and sometimes must even go without a pallet. If there are still some who, God forgive them, try to defend such abuse by an appeal to the words of Jesus, "For ye have the poor always with you" (Matt. 26:11), then out of respect for God's holy Word I must register my protest against such a misuse of the Scriptures. I invite those who so judge first to trace through the same Scriptures to see how the condition of the poor in Israel was almost luxurious compared to the misery in which our proletariat lies sunk.[3]

If you then ask me whether still more ought to be given, I answer without hesitation, most certainly. But I hasten to add that a charity which knows only how to give money is not yet Christian love. You will be free of guilt only when you also give your time, your energy, and your resourcefulness to help end such abuses for good, and when you allow nothing that lies hidden in the storehouse of your Christian religion to remain unused against the cancer that is destroying the vitality of our society in such alarming ways. For, indeed, the material need is appalling; the oppression is great. You do not honor God's Word if, in these circumstances, you ever forget how the Christ (just as his prophets before him and his apostles after him) invariably took sides *against* those who were powerful and living in luxury, and *for* the suffering and oppressed.

Even greater and more appalling is the spiritual need of our generation. When, in the midst of our social misery, I observe the demoralization that follows on the heels of material need, and hear a raucous voice which, instead of calling on the Father in heaven for salvation, curses God, mocks his Word, insults the cross of Golgotha, and tramples on whatever witness was still in the conscience—all in order to inflame everything wild and brutish in the human heart—then I stand before an abyss of spiritual misery that arouses my human compassion almost more than does the most biting poverty.

Out of this spiritual misery comes a cry of accusation against us as Christians. Were not almost all of these who now rage once baptized? And following their baptism, what did we sacrifice for them so that, instead of the caricature of the Christian religion against which they now utter their curse, they might understand something of God's real love in Christ Jesus? What have we Christians in the Netherlands done to stop this ravaging of the social life-blood by the poison of the French Revolution? When the infection became evident on the outside and social sickness took on an epidemic character, what did we on our side do to offer medicine and balm for its cure? Only now are we beginning to make our first weak attempt, in a social congress, to examine the death-struggle of society. By this time, our Christian thinkers should already have been laboring for twenty or thirty years with something of the earnestness and scholarly sense of a Marlo or a Schaeffle to plumb the depths of this desperate situation.[4]

Spiritual and Social Problems

There is so much damage to overcome! Simply consider the following problems.

Of primary significance is the problem of the majesty of our God, for, although I will come presently to concrete measures, we must first take up the general ideas that give shape and color to our entire conception of life. We are neither plant nor animal. Our rank and title is to be human. And, since we are human, we live first of all as conscious beings. Consequently, our feeling of happiness or unhappiness is in many respects dominated by our ideas, our general concepts. The first article of any social program that will bring salvation, therefore, must remain: "*I believe in God the Father Almighty, Maker of heaven and earth.*" This article is today being erased. Men refuse any longer to recognize God in statecraft. This is not because they do not find the poetry of religion charming, but because whoever says *I believe in God* thereby acknowledges God's ordering of nature and an ordinance of God above human conscience—a higher will to which we as creatures must submit ourselves. Today, everything must be a free creation of human art. The social structure must be planned entirely according to whim and caprice. God must go, so that without any natural bond to restrain them, men can turn every moral ordinance into its opposite and undermine every foundation of human society. Does this not provide a lesson for us? We as Christians must place the strongest possible emphasis on the majesty of God's authority and on the absolute validity of his ordinances, so that, even as we condemn the rotting social structure of our day, we will never try to erect any structure except one that rests on foundations laid by God.

Just as definitely, we as Christians must choose, in the second place, which side we will take in the controversy between state and society. He who, like the social democrats, would allow the state to be absorbed by society thereby denies the authority that God has established to maintain his majesty and his justice. Conversely, whoever would follow the state socialists and allow society to be absorbed by the state, carries incense for the deification of the state. He would put the state in place of God and allow the free society ordained by God to be destroyed. Against both of these, we as Christians must hold that state and society each has its own sphere, its own sovereignty, and that the social question cannot be resolved rightly unless we respect this duality and thus honor state authority as clearing the way for a free society.

In the third place, if asked whether our human society is an aggregate of individuals or an organic body, all those who are Christians must place themselves on the side of the social movement and against liberalism. As you know, God's Word teaches that we have all been created from one blood and joined in a single covenant through God. Both the solidarity of our guilt and the mystery of the reconciliation on Golgotha are absolutely incompatible with individualism and point instead to a struggle within the interconnected wholeness of our human society.

Moreover, if the pantheist, and by his inspiration the pessimist, would tell us that the course of history, fatal and miserable though it is, cannot be bro-

ken—that an iron fate rules the course of our human
life, and that we must first wade through this stream
of misery in order to emerge in later centuries in hap-
pier circumstances—then it is our duty as Christians,
with God's Word in hand, to oppose both this false
theory of destiny and this false system of culpable
passivity. Empowered by our confession of God's
providence, which also operates in the social arena to
separate good from evil, and taking in hand both
sword and trowel, we must simultaneously fight that
which is untenable and reinforce that which is obviously good.

If, in the fifth place, the furious zealot, fighting in
direct opposition to passive pessimism, seeks through
wild revolution to set fire to the house and to clear
the ground for an entirely new structure, then just as
definitely it becomes our calling as Christians, with
the apostolic word on our lips, to warn against all violation of authority and to oppose bravely every act of
force or lawlessness. In that case, we must make the
demand loudly and clearly that the course of our his-
toric development may be altered only through grad-
ual change and in a lawful way.[5]

In the sixth place, the social question raises the
issue of property. If one side contends that every concept of private property is absolute, and the other side
proposes to turn over all individual property to collective ownership, then the man who lives by God's
Word will here put forward the one true theory that
God gives in his ordinances. That truth is this: absolute property belongs only to God; all of our property

is on loan from him; our management is only stewardship. Therefore, on the one hand, only the Lord our God can discharge us from responsibility for that management; on the other hand, under God we have no right of rule except in the context of the organic association of mankind, and thus also in the context of the organic association of its possessions. What the social democrat calls "community of goods" never existed either in Israel or in the first Christian community. Such an absolute community of goods is excluded everywhere in Scripture. However, Scripture excludes just as completely every illusion of a right to dispose of one's property absolutely, as if one were God, without considering the needs of others.

Both the collectivist and those who advocate nationalization of land have made a separate issue of the ownership of land. We as Christians should neither arrogantly ridicule such ideas nor, as though God's Word gives us no guidance, shrug our shoulders at such a thorny problem. That kind of attitude is condemned in the first place by our conscience. We have heard how in Scotland three-fourths of the land is in the hands of fourteen persons, and how one of these fourteen recently bought a section in which forty-eight families lived and simply drove them off the land in order to extend his game preserve. Does not a voice in your innermost self tell you that such a disposal of land on which bread for the hungry must be grown cannot, as a matter of principle, be good, and that the lumping together of land ownership with individualistic ownership must run counter to God's ordinances? In the Lord's lawgiving for Israel you find a whole set of special regulations for the ownership of land. The fruitful field is given by God to *all the people* so that every tribe in Israel might dwell on it and live from it. Any agrarian regulation that does not reckon with this explicit ordinance ruins land and people.[6]

It is so profoundly false that God's Word lets us hear only calls for the salvation of our souls. No, God's Word gives us firm ordinances—even for our national existence and our common social life. It marks out clearly visible lines. We are unfaithful to God's Word if we fail to take notice of this fact and, for convenience sake, impiously permit our theory and practice to be determined by prevailing opinion or current law.[7]

The Power and Clarity of God's Word

On almost every point in regard to the social question, God's Word gives us the most positive direction. Think only of the family, whose immediate destruction is being advocated; of marriage, which some men would transpose into free love; of the family tie between generations, which some propose to dissolve by removing every right of inheritance; and not least, of birth, which others want to permit only by law and regulation. Did not Bilderdijk, still unacquainted with Malthus, denounce on the basis of God's Word all such agitation as "an ungodly thing, in opposition to God's positive ordinances, a murder of the unborn"?

For precisely the same reason, we must never, as long as we value God's Word, oppose colonization. God's earth, if cultivated, offers food enough for more than double the millions who now inhabit it. Is it not simply human folly to remain so piled up in a few small places on this planet that men must crawl away into cellars and slums, while at the same time there are other places a hundred times larger than our native land, awaiting the plow and the sickle, or on which herds of the most valuable cattle wander without an owner? "Be fruitful," says the divine ordinance, but also "replenish the earth" (Gen.1:28)—and don't overcrowd the small area within your narrow boundaries. Indeed, the institution of marriage, which is damaged by such cramped geography, must always be held high in honor by Christians. God punishes us with every curse of the sins of sensuality and prostitution when we oppose his regulation in this matter.

By that same Word of God, the family is portrayed as the wonderful creation through which the rich fabric of our organic human life must spin itself out. Here also you need not hesitate. You know what you have to do. We do not have to organize society; we have only to develop the germ of organization that God himself has created in our human nature. Away with false individualism, therefore, and anathema on every attempt to break up the family. At least in our Dutch state, which has now for three centuries felt, in flowering family life, the tensile spring of its power, may the loosening of this basic foundation never, at least with our permission, be allowed.

It is no different with work. Specifically with an eye to physical labor (which must come up for strong consideration in conjunction with the social question), the divine ordinance speaks: "In the sweat of thy face shalt thou eat bread" (Gen. 3:19). Next to it stands this: "the laborer is worthy of his hire" (Luke 10:7). You shall not defraud him of his wage, much less withhold it from him (see James 5:4). The Lord says specifically through Moses, "Thou shalt not oppress an hired servant that is poor and needy" (Deut. 24:14), and do not hold back his wage (Lev. 19:13; Deut. 24:15). You shall honor the laborer as a fellow-man, of one blood with you, for to degrade him to a mere instrument is to alienate your own brother (see Mal. 2:10). The worker, too, must be able to live as a person created in the image of God. He must be able to fulfill his calling as man and father. The worker has a soul to lose; he must be able to serve his God. For that reason he has a right to a Sabbath—a right especially important for the one whose work tends to pull him down to a material level. God created this worker as a frail creature, as one whose strength can be broken through sickness and accident—a strength that also decreases with age. After he can no longer toil, he too should be able to eat the bread earned in his days of vigor.

So speaks God in his Word, and your worker reads that too. He must and may read it, and when he reads it, does not God's Word itself give him the right—true, not to grumble, much less to rebel, but at any rate—to complain and to indict a social arrangement which so painfully deprives him of that which divine mercy has ordained for him? Although this suffering does not oppress most of us personally, should it not weigh upon us for the sake of our brothers? Have we ever the right to cease delivering, with God's Word in hand, a withering critique of such an unhealthy society? Indeed, regardless of the degree of state intervention, have we any right to rest as long as this society remains unreformed according to God's Word? To mistreat the workman as a "piece of machinery" is and remains a violation of his human dignity. Even worse, it is a sin directly contrary to the sixth commandment: You shall not kill the worker socially.[8]

Finally, a brief word about state aid. God the Lord unmistakably instituted the basic rule for the duty of government. Government exists to administer his justice on earth, and to uphold that justice. The tasks of family and society therefore lie outside government's jurisdiction. With those it is not to meddle. But as soon as there is any clash among the different spheres of life, where one sphere trespasses on or violates the domain which by divine ordinance belongs to the other, then it is the God-given duty of government to uphold justice before arbitrariness, and to withstand, by the justice of God, the physical superiority of the stronger. What it may not do is to grant such assurance of justice to one sphere and withhold it from another. A code for business (I still adhere to what I said in 1875 to the States-General) calls also for a code for labor. The government should help labor obtain justice. Labor must also be allowed to organize itself independently in order to defend its rights.

As for the other type of state aid—namely, the distribution of money—it is certain that such intervention is not excluded in Israel's lawgiving, but there it is held to a minimum. Therefore I say that, unless you wish to undermine the position of the laboring class and destroy its natural resilience, the material assistance of the state should be confined to an absolute minimum. The continuing welfare of people and nation, including labor, lies only in powerful individual initiative.[9]

So then, there is no need of further argument to show that the outlook on human life furnished by the Christian religion establishes, for an approach to all parts of the social question, an unwavering point of departure from which to attempt concrete solutions to each problem. We do not stumble around in the dark. The principles by which we are obliged to test the existing situation and existing juridical relationships lie clearly expressed in the Word of God. We fall short in our duty as Christian citizens if we shirk the serious task of reconstructing whatever is manifestly in conflict with the ordinance of God.

A Balanced Perspective

Having said all this, however, I may not stop here. For even if we pursue this path of justice to its very end, the goal that God has in view will never be reached by means of legal measures designed to improve social conditions. Rules alone will not cure our sick society; the medicine must also reach the *heart* of rich and poor. Sin is such a tremendous power that it mocks all your dikes and sluices, and in spite of your legal regulations, it will again and again flood the field of human life with the waters of its passion and selfishness.

So I return to the point at which I began earlier. Because we are conscious beings, almost everything depends on the standard of values which our consciousness constructs. If this present life is all there is, then I can understand that a man would desire to enjoy it before he dies, and would find the mystery of suffering wholly insoluble. Therefore, it is your calling, confessors of our Lord Jesus Christ, to place *life eternal* in the foreground for both rich and poor, and to do so with a gripping and soul-piercing earnestness. Only he who reckons with eternal life knows the real price of this earthly life. If external possession, if material good, if sensual pleasure is the whole of what is intended for man, then I can understand the materialist and do not see how I could properly reprimand the Epicurean. Therefore, it is your duty, children of the kingdom, to seize every occasion and means to impress on rich and poor that the peace of God is a much richer and holier treasure, and that the spiritual welfare of man is of much higher worth.

On the social question too, what is really at issue is how contentment and happiness may rule. This by no means depends only on the amount of your possessions, but first of all on the need that is aroused within you and on the *kind* of need that calls for gratification. If the socialist repeats the slander that this is a dismissal of the poor with "pie in the sky," the facts contradict him. Whoever is not a stranger to our Christian families, even of the lowest classes, knows how much the fear of our God can do for those who have only a meager portion of worldly goods. He will have observed how that little portion, which elsewhere would be dissipated in alcoholism and sin, receives in the case of Christian laborers a double blessing. He can testify how even in a poor household human dignity reveals its true colors in husband, wife, and children. He will have thanked God for the bountiful share of a happy life and joyful heart that is theirs despite their limited means. These who are the backbone of the laboring class do not ask, they do not beg. Rather, they sometimes lend a helping hand to those who receive less than themselves.

Therefore, it is my most fervent conviction that every prophet who sets himself up among our people and undermines these fundamental elements of popular consciousness is guilty of cruel and merciless behavior. Similarly, the modernistic tendency to sow the seed of doubt about our eternal destiny from the pulpit must also be branded as cruel. No less cruel is our public school, which has dragged the children of our people down from this lofty standpoint. By contrast, it is impossible to overestimate what our Christian school has already done for the suffering of our people, even if it has done no more than return to thousands of families this single dependable criterion for our human life, our human good, and our human enjoyment.

For those of us more liberally endowed, all of our life, too, should be a single unbroken pronouncement of these holy principles. You who have received more may not wantonly fling these principles in the faces of the poor through your immoderate attachment to earthly goods—by giving the impression that enjoyment of luxury means more to you than anything else. Far worse, you should not grudgingly, with a heavy heart, distribute in the name of the Lord what you have received from him as your landlord. For then the less fortunate has no faith in your preaching, and he is right. Every man's inner sense of truth rebels against a theory of eternal happiness that serves only to keep Lazarus at a distance here on earth.

There cannot be two different faiths—one for you and one for the poor. The question on which the whole social problem really pivots is whether you recognize in the less fortunate, even in the poorest, not merely a creature, a person in wretched circumstances, but one of your own flesh and blood: for the sake of Christ, *your brother*. It is exactly this noble sentiment that, sad to say, has been weakened and dulled in such a provoking manner by the materialism of this century. There are men of wealth, as you know, who have become alarmed at the threat of social democracy and now, from fear of this threat, grasp for relief measures none of them thought about before. But at least in this circle of those who confess the Lord, I pray that you will allow a more perfect love to drive out all such fear. For those who are diverted by fear for their money box have no place marching in the ranks with us. This is holy ground, and he who would walk on it must first loosen the sandals of his egotism. The only sound permitted here is the stirring and eloquent voice of the merciful Samaritan whispering in our ears. There is suffering round about you, and those who suffer are your brothers, sharers of your nature, your own flesh and blood. You might have been in their place and they in your more pleasant position.

The gospel speaks to you of a Redeemer who, although he was rich, became poor for your sake so he might make you rich. The gospel leads you to kneel down in worship before a child born to us, but born in a stable, laid down in a manger, and wrapped in swaddling clothes. It points you to God's Son, but one who became the *Son of Man* and went through the country, from wealthy Judea to the poorer, despised Galilee, addressing himself to those who were in need or oppressed by sorrow. Yes, it tells you that this singular Savior, before he left this earth, stooped before his disciples in the clothes of a slave, washed their feet one by one, and then stood and said, "For I have given you an example, that ye should do as I have done to you" (John 13:15).

Time for Action

The tremendous love springing up from God within you displays its radiance not in the fact that you allow poor Lazarus to quiet his hunger with the crumbs that fall from your overburdened table. All such charity is more like an insult to the manly heart that beats in the bosom of the poor man. Rather, the love within you displays its radiance in this: Just as rich and poor sit down with each other at the communion table, so also you feel for the poor man as for a member of the body, which is all that you are as well. To the poor man, a loyal handshake is often sweeter than a bountiful largess. A friendly word, not spoken haughtily, is the gentlest balm for one who weeps over his wounds. Divine compassion, sympathy, a suffering *with* us and *for* us—that was the mystery of Golgotha. You, too, must suffer with your suffering brothers. Only then will the holy music of consolation vibrate in your speech. Then, driven by this sympathy of compassion, you will naturally conform your action to your speech.

For *deeds* of love are indispensable. Obviously, the poor man cannot wait until the restortation of our social structure has been completed. Almost certainly he will not live long enough to see that happy day. Nevertheless, he still has to live; he must feed his hungry mouth and the mouths of his hungry family. Therefore, vigorous help is necessary. However highly I am inclined to praise your willingness to make sacrifices—and this is possible through God's grace to many of you—nevertheless, the holy art of "giving for Jesus' sake" ought to be much more strongly developed among us Christians. Never forget that all state relief for the poor is a blot on the honor of your Savior.[10]

So, have sympathy for the suffering of the depressed and oppressed. In nothing so strongly as in this holy suffering can you be "followers of God as beloved children." In that holy motive of compassion hides the entire secret of the heavenly power that you as Christians can exercise. When the impulse to assist the poor—through advice, leadership, and your own initiative—is awakened within you, then you will not be embarrassed to ask for helpers. You will find all who are Christian, not merely in *name* but also in *reality*, vying for the high honor of assisting in this service of mercy to your suffering brothers in Christ's name.

Men and brothers, may our Congress be governed by this high and holy motive. Let none of us boast of the good work to which we here commit ourselves; rather, let there be a quiet sense of shame that we have not met before. May we find a peaceful symbol in the happy fact that men representing labor are meeting here and deliberating with fellow Christians from the higher classes. In that symbol may we be able to anticipate fulfillment of the inviting prophecy that Christian confidence will soon be perfectly restored among us.

If you ask me finally whether I really dare build any hope on this Congress—hope that we shall at least come somewhat closer to solving the burning question of the day—do not forget that the social need is a world problem. The social question has an *international* character, and therefore can never be really settled within the narrow confines of our small nation. We may lack the power to determine what the future will bring in this respect. It could be that our long-provoked God in his just judgment has destined very anxious days for us, if not immediately, then in the near future. These are hidden things, which at this Congress we leave to the Lord our God. But while awaiting whatever may come, there remains for us his revealed injunction to do at this Congress whatever our hands find to do, and do it with all our might. May God the Lord add his benediction to that end.

Furthermore, if rescue is yet to appear for our violently disturbed society, then our fast-dying century must recognize Christ as its Savior. I close, therefore, with a prayer, a prayer that I know lives in the heart of each of you, that even if this rescue should be delayed, and even if the stream of unrighteousness must rise still higher, may it never be possible to say of the Christians of the Netherlands that through our fault, through the lukewarmness of our Christian faith, whether in higher or lower classes, the rescue of our society was hindered and the blessing of the God of our fathers forfeited.

Notes

Introduction

1. On late nineteenth-century social conditions and political ideologies in Europe and America in general, see Bob Goudzwaard, *Capitalism and Progress: A Diagnosis of Western Society*, trans. and ed. Josina Van Nuis Zylstra (Toronto: Wedge; Grand Rapids: Eerdmans, 1979), pp. 80–117; Carl N. Degler, *The Age of the Economic Revolution, 1876–1900* (Glenview, Ill.: Scott, Foresman, 1967); Wolfgang J. Mommensen, ed., *The Emergence of the Welfare State in Britain and Germany, 1850–1950* (London: Croom Helm, 1981); James T. Kloppenberg, *Uncertain Victory: Social Democracy and Progressivism in European and American Thought, 1870–1920* (New York: Oxford University Press, 1986), pp. 199–297.

2. Kuyper mentions these different Christian responses at the beginning of his speech. Two constructive introductions and assessments, both in Dutch, which situate Kuyper's efforts in the larger context are A. Kouwenhoven, *De Dynamiek van Christelijk Sociaal Denken* (Nijkerk: Callenbach, 1989), pp. 32–94; and H. E. S. Woldring and D. Th. Kuiper, *Reformatorische Maatschappijkritiek* (Kampen: J. H. Kok, 1980). Leo XIII's *Rerum novarum* can be found in David M. Byers, ed., *Justice in the Marketplace: Collected Statements of the Vatican and the United*

States Catholic Bishops on Economic Policy, 1891–1984 (Washington, D.C.: U.S. Catholic Conference, 1985), pp. 9–41.

On the broader context of emerging, organized Christian responses to economic, social, and political changes in Europe, see Michael P. Fogarty, *Christian Democracy in Western Europe, 1820–1953* (Westport, Conn.: Greenwood, 1974 [1957]; Hans Maier, *Revolution and Church: The Early History of Christian Democracy, 1789–1901*, trans. Emily M. Schossberger (Notre Dame: Notre Dame University Press, 1969 [1965]); Eric O. Hanson, *The Catholic Church in World Politics* (Princeton: Princeton University Press, 1987), esp. pp. 19–161; Suzanne Berger, ed., *Religion in Western European Politics* (London: Frank Cass, 1982); John McManners, *Church and State in France, 1870–1914* (London: SPCK, 1972); W. O. Shanahan, *German Protestants Face the Social Question* (Notre Dame: University of Notre Dame Press, 1954); Joseph N. Moody, ed., *Church and Society: Catholic Social and Political Thought and Movements, 1789–1950* (New York: Arts, 1953); M. Einaudi and F. Goguel, *Christian Democracy in Italy and France* (Notre Dame: University of Notre Dame Press, 1952); and Amintore Fanfani, *Catholicism, Protestantism, and Capitalism* (Notre Dame: University of Notre Dame Press, 1984 [1935]).

3. One book-length biography of Kuyper in English is by Frank VandenBerg, *Abraham Kuyper* (St. Catherines, Ont.: Paideia, 1978 [1960]). Essays with biographical material include James D. Bratt, "Abraham Kuyper's Public Career," *Reformed Journal* (Oct. 1987): 9–12; idem, "Raging Tumults of the Soul: The Private Life of Abraham Kuyper," *Reformed Journal* (Nov. 1987): 9–13; McKendree R. Langley, *The Practice of Political Spirituality: Episodes from the Public Career of Abraham Kuyper, 1879–1918* (Jordan Station, Ont.: Paideia, 1984); and Justus M. Van der Kroef, "Abraham Kuyper and the Rise of Neo-Calvinism in the Netherlands," *Church History* 17 (1948): 316–34.

4. The best introduction to Groen van Prinsterer is Harry Van Dyke's *Groen van Prinsterer's Lectures on Unbelief and Revolution* (Jordan Station, Ont.: Wedge, 1989), which both details Groen's life and work as well as translates his most influential book—the Lectures.

5. On Kuyper's political career and its relation to the Anti-Revolutionary party and Dutch political history, see Langley, *Practice of Political Spirituality*; James W. Skillen and Stanley W. Carlson-Thies, "Religion and Political Development in Nineteenth-Century Holland," *Publius* (Summer 1982): 43–64; Hans Daalder, "The Netherlands: Opposition in a Segmented Society," in Robert A. Dahl, ed., *Political Oppositions in Western Democracies* (New Haven: Yale University Press, 1966), pp. 200ff.; Dirk Jellema, "Abraham Kuyper's Attack on Liberalism," *Review of Politics* 19 (1957): 472–85; Johan G. Westra, "Confessional Political Parties in the Netherlands, 1813–1946" (Ph.D. diss., University of Michigan, 1972); and Steven E. Meyer, "Calvinism and the Rise of the Protestant Political Movement in the Netherlands" (Ph.D. diss., Georgetown University, 1976).

6. Three Dutch works on the Free University of Amsterdam and Kuyper's role in it are M. Van Os and W. J. Wieringa, eds., *Wetenschap and Rekenschap, 1880–1980* (Kampen: J. H. Kok, 1980); G. Puchinger, *Honderd Jaar Vrije Universieit* (Delft: W. D. Meinema, 1980); and J. Stellingwerff, *Kuyper en de VU* (Kampen: J. H. Kok, 1987).

7. Abraham Kuyper, *Lectures on Calvinism* (Grand Rapids: Eerdmans, 1961 [1931, 1898]).

8. See, for example, Kuyper's *The Work of the Holy Spirit*, trans. Henri De Vries (New York: Funk and Wagnalls, 1908); *His Decease at Jerusalem*, trans. John Hendrik de Vries (Grand Rapids: Eerdmans, 1925); *Keep Thy Solemn Feasts*, trans. John Hendrik de Vries (Grand Rapids: Eerdmans, 1928); and *The Revelation of St. John*, trans. John Hendrik de Vries (Grand Rapids: Eerdmans, 1963 [1935]).

9. One chapter in Kuyper's *Lectures on Calvinism* is on politics (pp. 78–109). Introductory expositions of his political and social philosophy can be found in James W. Skillen, "The Development of Calvinistic Political Theory in the Netherlands" (Ph.D. diss., Duke University, 1974); and S. U. Zuidema, "Common Grace and Christian Action in Abraham Kuyper," in idem, *Communication and Confrontation* (Toronto: Wedge, 1972), pp. 52–105.

10. Quoted in the introductory biographical note by John Hendrik de Vries to Kuyper's *Lectures on Calvinism*, p. vii.

11. See especially Kuyper, *Lectures on Calvinism*, pp. 9–77; and Zuidema, "Common Grace and Christian Action," pp. 88–101.

12. See Kuyper, *Lectures on Calvinism*; idem, "Sphere Sovereignty," forthcoming in James W. Skillen and Rockne McCarthy, eds., *Political Order and the Plural Structure of Society* (Atlanta: Emory University Law and Religion Program, 1991); and Herman Dooyeweerd, *Roots of Western Culture: Pagan, Secular, and Christian Options*, trans. John Kraay (Toronto: Wedge, 1979), pp. 40–60.

Part 1

1. We must admit, to our shame, that the Roman Catholics are far ahead of us in their study of the social problem. Indeed, very far ahead. The action of the Roman Catholics should spur us to show more dynamism. The encyclical *Rerum novarum* of Leo XIII states the principles which are common to all Christians, and which we share with our Roman Catholic compatriots.

2. Groen van Prinsterer warned the [Parliamentary] Chamber on June 18, 1850: "It is the misfortune of our age that men isolate democracy. It will do us no good simply to give power to the middle classes. They too are a *new aristocracy* and a new privileged class, and it will amount to only a minor change." That Groen expected improvement only from a better *organization* of society is clear from the following: "Probably the worst evil is pauperism. Poverty, no work; broken relationships between the higher and lower classes; no relationship recognized except that of work and pay; proletariat and capitalist. What will develop from this? That is uncertain, but the source from which all this has developed is not uncertain. It has grown from the French Revolution's idea of freedom and equality."

3. This constant appeal of the socialists to Christ must be neither underestimated nor valued too highly. A double motive is at work here. First, it is a means of propaganda, for men know how easily they win influence as long as they appeal to Scripture. But

second, it is a matter of mistaken conviction. Some socialists are indeed impressed by the strong contrast between the way in which Christ saw the social need and the attitude toward that need adopted through long years by many Christians. In both of these lies hidden an awareness of the authority exercised only by the Scripture, and that is a happy sign.

4. The error frequently committed is this: men associate the Christian religion only with the world of feeling. Undoubtedly even in this respect its significance for the social problem is great, insofar as much depends on the state of feeling in rich and poor, in rulers and subjects, and in public interpreters and spokesmen. He who can contribute even a little to improve the feeling does thereby an excellent work. But it is a mutilation of the Christian religion to confine its working to the area of emotional life. Christianity professes not only Christ, but the Triune God—Father, Son, and Holy Spirit. The Creed therefore begins: "I believe in God, the Father Almighty, Maker of heaven and earth." In this there is the explicit affirmation that the Christian religion must have a conviction regarding our relation to nature, authority, and fellow-men, and must also include a view of human nature and its attributes. In other words, Christianity holds a conviction regarding just those phenomena which together determine the social question.

5. Only from this point of view does one understand the French Revolution simultaneously in its appalling necessity and in its deeply sinful character. Statecraft had gradually led the nations down impassable paths and had done such violence to human nature and society that a reaction was inexorably necessary. To that extent a terrible explosion was due, and to that extent the French Revolution was indeed a righteous judgment of God on those who had misused the authority and power entrusted to them. But this in no way lessens the deeply sinful character of the French Revolution, insofar as, contrary to God's ordinances, it separated nature from history, and substituted the will of the *individual* for the will of the *Creator of nations*. This now stamps it as a movement opposed in principle to God and his Christ, and, for that reason, after a short breathing spell, it brought about a corruption deadlier than the corruption the French revolted against in 1789.

6. The fault of many a Bible reader and many a preacher is that he reads or discusses such moving words as these without applying them directly to the reality of his own environment.

7. If words as strong as these were not found in the Bible, and if anyone should dare pen them now on his own initiative, people would brand him a crypto-socialist. For those who hope for money and who would build on the power of money, the Holy Scripture is a despairing book. The Holy Spirit who speaks in Scripture finds an abundance of gold and silver to be dangerous rather than desirable, and deems an inheritance of millions not even distantly to be compared with the inheritance that awaits us as saints. This is the witness of the Lord in his Word, and I may not represent it otherwise. Let no one reproach me for it, but let him realize that his criticism directly attacks the Bible itself.

Part 2

1. One cannot pay enough attention to the parallel between the social life that preceded the fall of the Roman state and the social injustices of our time. Of course, the culture was different then, but the contrast was the same. If the press had existed at that time, and if the newspapers had survived, journalists today would be able to copy whole sections from them. The moral props of that society were mildewed and rotted, even as now. Roman civilization, excelling in refinement, finally collapsed. So, too, our Western civilization will eventually succumb, unless the Christian religion, which is now a vital power, intervenes to redeem it.

2. This can be explained only by the fact that scholarly and cultured men began by undermining faith in life after death, and then went on to destroy it. Doubt is no beginning for faith, and to speak merely of a "hope of immortality" is the same as denying faith in an eternal existence, at least for the great mass of people. I consider this cruel. For although the socialists do not believe in eternal life, neither can they prove the opposite.

3. That this unity in the name of the Father actually exists is clear from Malachi 2:10, where the prophet asks in the name of the Lord, "Have we not all one Father? hath not one God created us? why do we deal treacherously every man against his brother, by profaning the covenant of our fathers?" The same thing is also clearly asserted in the Lord's Prayer. In every Lord's Prayer the poor prays for the rich that God may give him his bread for that day, and the rich prays it for the poor. Nowhere in this prayer is there a "my" or an "I" but always "we" and "us."

4. To be treasurer is always dangerous. From money there proceeds an ignoble influence on our heart; hence it is unhealthy for a people when banking techniques and the stock exchange become dominant; hence it is precisely the man of high finance for whom the chance to learn to bow humbly before his God is so remote. Bilderdijk realized this when he wrote Da Costa: "The fact that those who are by profession merchants and gamblers have no Christianity is self-explanatory."

5. Jesus flattered no one, neither rich nor poor, but put both in their place. Exactly on this account Jesus occupies so eminent a position. With our men of influence you generally find either scorn for the poor and flattery of the rich, or abuse of the rich and flattery of the poor. This is in conflict with the Christian religion. *Both* must be convicted of their sin. But this fact remains: Scripture, when it corrects the poor, does so much more tenderly and gently; and in contrast, when it calls the rich to account, it uses much harsher words. Yet our poor also fall away from their faith if they build their hopes on all kinds of help from the state, and not solely on their Father who is in heaven.

6. It is noteworthy that the church was organized not only to seek the eternal welfare of its followers, but also to remove social injustices. Exactly because of its divine simplicity, this organization brought forth a double fruit. It follows that the church forsakes its principle when it is only concerned with heaven and does not relieve earthly need, and it also follows that our diaconates will have to function very differently if they truly want to honor Christ.

7. In this connection it certainly may not be forgotten that the voluntary poverty of the monastics attempted to continue the original tradition; and to that extent this vow remains a well

intentioned protest against the secularization of the church. But, ignoring the question of whether these vows were actually permissible, the fact is that the monasteries of that age progressively fictionalized the "vow of poverty." And even had they remained more true to their ideal, the monastics could never have made amends for the immeasurable damage the church itself inflicted on social relationships by its seeking of worldly splendor. As long as the church was persecuted, it flourished, and it ennobled social relations. When it came into a position of honor under Constantine, it paid for the honor with its moral influence, and consequently ended up throwing its weight on the side of the balance exactly opposite where Jesus had placed it.

Part 3

1. This is the pivot on which the whole social question turns. The French Revolution, like present-day liberalism, was antisocial, and the social need that now disturbs Europe is the evil fruit of the individualism enthroned by the French Revolution.

2. It is just as one-sided to try to explain social injustices almost exclusively by the machine and steam power as it is to shut one's eyes to these influences. Too much stress is commonly laid on the machine. If personal faith and the moral life of society had not been so defiantly undermined by the French Revolution, the class struggle would never have taken on such formidable proportions. The machine and steam power simply confront us with a tension. On the one hand, steam tools improved the lot of the worker and relieved him of drudgery. On the other hand, the endless division of labor dulls the spirit, while the machine lowers the value of hand labor and, since it can do the work of a hundred men, sets ninety-nine breadless on the streets.

3. This change is most apparent in the entirely different outlooks on life found in the great cities and the rural areas. It explains why the lower rural classes, even though their condition is often more wretched than that of the lower urban classes, actually live much more happily and complain much less.

4. This fact simply cannot be denied. Inevitably, capital absorbs more and more capital until it meets a power of resistance it cannot break. That resistance is, in the present context, the impossibility of the worker remaining alive. And, whatever else one may say, Lasalle is perfectly correct in saying that this brazen law of iron necessity is the curse of our society. This law is a spontaneous consequence of laissez faire, of absolutely free competition. Capital absorbs more capital in this way not because of any evil purpose, but simply because it does not meet with any other power of resistance short of the "to be or not to be" of the worker—the instrument of capital-nourishment.

5. I willingly recognize the earnest efforts that liberalism has made toward the improvement of the lower class. But what did it offer them? Reading, writing, and arithmetic! And what did it take away from them? Faith, the courage to live, and a moral dynamic. What did it withhold from them? Trade schools and a share in capital.

6. In this respect, our store displays do more evil than people think. In various ways they stimulate covetousness and create needs that if not eventually satisfied leave behind a feeling of bitter discontent. So also the excessive luxury of our schools has done harm to a class that at home can never live on such a footing. Happiness is not an *absolute* but a *relative* concept. He who awakens needs he is not able to satisfy lays a great responsibility on himself and commits an act of unmerciful cruelty.

7. It is not enough to say that the social-democratic movement issues from liberal theory; it must also be stressed that the liberal makes an arbitrary stop on a road that, in accord with his own system, has to be pursued. He is not only related in spirit to the social democrat, but over against the social democrat he is in the wrong, because of his arbitrariness, egoism, and inconsistency.

8. It is indeed strange how many of the ordinary citizens in our land simultaneously reject this advocacy of force on the part of the social democrats and yet praise the French Revolution so highly. It surely won't do to say that the September murders were merely *excesses*; for without *revolution* there would have been no Revolution in 1789. Every liberal, even if one does not hold the excesses against him, thus takes responsibility for the

revolutionary use of force. It amounts to this, that force is considered lawful when used to the advantage of the liberals, but is detested the moment it tends to undermine their own power.

9. One should keep these essential characteristics of the social question well in mind. Our implication is not that the structure must be wholly destroyed and an entirely new order set up in place of the old society. Rather, the right of history always remains valid, and there is no possibility of complete demolition. Even though one imagines that he does it, he does not do it. History's influence is too powerful. On the other hand, one may not say that everything is finished if one only puts on a few dabs of paint and replaces a shingle here and there.

10. We do not say here that the religious and philanthropic aspects of the problem are not important, but only that one who sees no further and senses no more than this is not even in contact with the social question.

11. Rouge does not cure the dullness of your skin, but aggravates the sickliness of your complexion. So it is with our society. It lives in more refined forms; it clothes itself more stylishly but not more beautifully; it pretends to be glowing with youth. But he who is not a stranger in the boudoir of our social life, and sometimes sees this matron in her negligee, knows all too well how faded and pale is her real appearance.

12. The beautiful word "*social*" should not be considered the private preserve of social democrats. Christianity is preeminently entitled to the term. The beautiful picture of the church's social character given to us by the holy apostle Paul (1 Cor. 12:12–27, Eph. 4:16) is, if we make the necessary allowances, applicable also to our human society. Rightly viewed, it must even be professed that in the church of Christ the original organism of humanity, now purified, lives again.

13. The social question can only be solved internationally, but before the several states see this and dare to act with the required energy, more *particularism* will have to be overcome than perhaps can be done without a general combustion in all of Europe. We are now moving in the direction that each state, socially speaking, is thinking only of itself, and economically each state begins to live at war with the others, at most seeking salvation through a narrow coalition with a few allies.

14. Nothing is more foolish than to see in the social question only a passing storm or a fleeting cloud. It is perfectly true that the socialists are mutually divided, and that they do not as yet have leaders who are disinterested and eminent enough to call worldwide action into existence. Their congresses are mostly dramas of tumult, their press overflows with invective. But you are surely mistaken if, for that reason, you hold the social question to be a temporary inconvenience. On the contrary, precisely this fact—that the socialists, in spite of their many differences, have made such giant strides forward—indicates the vigorous impetus that propagates social democracy. Do not forget that the Internationale was instituted as recently as 1864 and shortly thereafter fell in ruins; that the new association is still faulty in many respects; and that nevertheless, after only a quarter-century, the social movement has already set all Europe agog.

15. We do not deny here that greed and envy play a very great role in the social question. As persons, the members of the class now complaining are no better than the men of the class that is satisfied. He who was poor and becomes rich usually turns away from socialism. On the other hand, there are no more dangerous socialists than the people who have lost their fortunes. But evil passion cannot call to life a lasting world movement. The power of socialism stems not from covetous desire, but rather from the moral demand of societal life. This demand speaks to the conscience; here lies its life blood; on this demand religion places its seal; and the question of private property only comes hobbling up at the rear of this unavoidably righteous demand.

16. The same pantheism that wipes out all differences in the moral realm, that dares place Nero next to Jesus as an equally interesting temporal phenomenon, leads in the sociological arena to the dullest and most cynical fatalism. For the pessimist the situation is wretched, but there is no way to improve it: we glide along the decline until we sink in the depths. All this is our destiny. On the rubbish of our civilization we may perhaps begin a new building. Perhaps? But these pessimists know nothing of the eternal dynamic that lies hidden in the heart of the Christian nations, and which can rise above that which spelled ruin for Babylon, Athens, and Rome.

Part 4

1. The ancient problem of the One and the many recurs here. The *starting point* of both the social democrats and the liberals is individualistic, in the individual person, and thus in Pelagian free will. That the dynamic of the French Revolution also works very decidedly in the social democrats is clear from the continually recurring demand that mature male individuals shall rule the affairs of state and society by majority vote. They do not even understand our demand that the starting point should be in the *family*.

2. Bilderdijk expresses himself very strongly. He says: "There is nothing else to do but to restore the citizen-state to its former scope. If there is ground, let men cultivate it. Where there is shipping or fishery, let men expand them. If these three are not enough, provide industrial work, and see that everyone can find work, and that through this work a man can find bread for his wife and children. Work should be the aim; let there be free and compulsory factories, free and compulsory farms. Let honor be attached to the free and shame to the compulsory labor. Let no one who says he is available lack work, and let no beggary be tolerated. Land, seafaring, fishery, industry—these will support the workers, and no more is needed. Whoever aims at profit therein is driven by a wrong spirit.

"All is tainted because instead of making money simply a means in society, men have turned it into the chief object, purpose, and end. As long as men do this, misery endures and increases more and more. This is the great plague that has gone out over Europe, and only those who have the seal of God on their forehead and rest in his providence are immune, and do not pray or work for money, but despise it. These few do indeed suffer, but God feeds them.

"All nations of Europe serve this Mammon, and their only recovery lies in overthrowing the false system. There is nothing more to say. [The fact that there is] no bread for those who are willing to work is in conflict with the basic law of all work: 'In the sweat of thy face shalt thou eat bread' (Gen. 3:19)."

3. The words of John 12:8, "For the poor always ye have with you," give no rule, but merely state a fact. There is no implica-

tion that it *should* be so, but at most that such will be the case. Second, it will not do to conclude from this statement that Jesus is giving a prophecy about *later* ages. In the third place, we often completely overlook the reproach that hides in these words. The Greek actually means not "with you," but "in life as you are patterning it, you will always have the poor." This was said to Judas and his like, men who carry the purse and use it like Judas.

4. Too much stress cannot be laid on this. There must also be on our side *study* and *work*. We will get further with the social question neither by sentimental talk nor by shallow generalities. This was the fault of the earlier communists, and of utopia-seekers such as Fourier and Proudhon. It is precisely in study and thorough research that the very serious power of socialism lies.

5. Revolution and history stand only partly opposed to each other. History knows, besides the regular process, the *disturbance* of this process through violence. Against revolution as principle and as fact there is defense only in the apostolic word, "Submit yourselves to every ordinance of man for the Lord's sake" (1 Pet. 2:13). And then also, according to the Calvinistic interpretation, this passivity finds its limit only in the demand of God's Word.

6. It does not follow from this that our salvation lies in nationalization of the land, but whoever superciliously mocks all such plans and ideas and brands them as socialistic is guilty of superficiality and unbelief. Agrarian regulation is always most difficult. Compare Henry George's *Progress and Poverty* (1879).

7. The Bible gives us not only *ideas* but also definite *rules*, and Christians who say they bow down before God's Word but go along with the men of the French Revolution in their social and political ideas are not integrated men; they lead an ambiguous life. They manifestly do not fully realize the power of the Scriptures and the Word.

8. Work also is an ordinance of God, one that is primarily governed by the question of how we should view the worker. The answer to that question reads this way: We should view the worker as a human being, created in the image of God, destined for eternal life, and here called to stand as man and father in society, and to share with us the vicissitudes of sickness and health, youth, maturity, and old age. Cardinal Newman and Pope Leo

XIII correctly agree with this. We shall not be satisfied with the structure of society until it offers all human beings an existence worthy of man. Until then, the structure must remain the object of our criticism. But one should not seek salvation in monetary help from the state. That is always offensive to human feelings and also weakens our national strength. The help that the state must give is *better legislation*.

9. The Antirevolutionary party [Kuyper's party] must see to it that it does not permit itself to be drawn along by state socialism. Even though we stand directly opposed to the individualism of the Liberal party, we nevertheless wholeheartedly subscribe to the warning given by Goshen, which Leon Say translates thus: "If we have learned anything from history, we should be able to say that the self-assurance of the individual and the respect of the state for natural liberty are necessary conditions for statehood, the prosperity of society, and the greatness of a people." Along these lines the whole Antirevolutionary program is set up. It would indeed be safest to unite all our strength in the organization of labor and labor contracts.

10. It is perfectly true that if no help is forthcoming from elsewhere the state must help. We may let no one starve from hunger as long as bread lies molding in so many cupboards. And when the state intervenes, it must do so quickly and sufficiently.